This Book Belongs To

_____

OUR BOOK RANGE

For more visit

www.grantpublishingltd.com

Book design and editing by Josephine Grant

40 Facts About Botswana

Grant Publishing

Bite-sized facts and stunning photographs about the wonderful country that is Botswana. A great choice to introduce your child to the world around them.

40 Facts About Botswana

Let's learn something

Botswana is a country in the continent of Africa.

Three Dikgosi Monument, Gaborone, Botswana

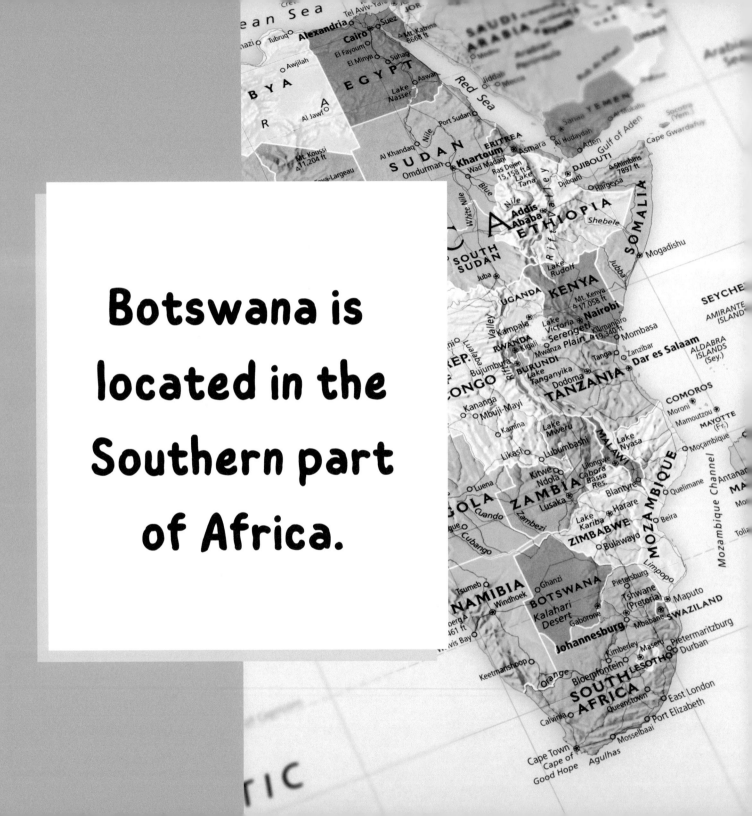

Botswana is located in the Southern part of Africa.

Botswana is officially the Republic of Botswana.

Botswana

Botswana is a landlocked country.

Okavango Delta

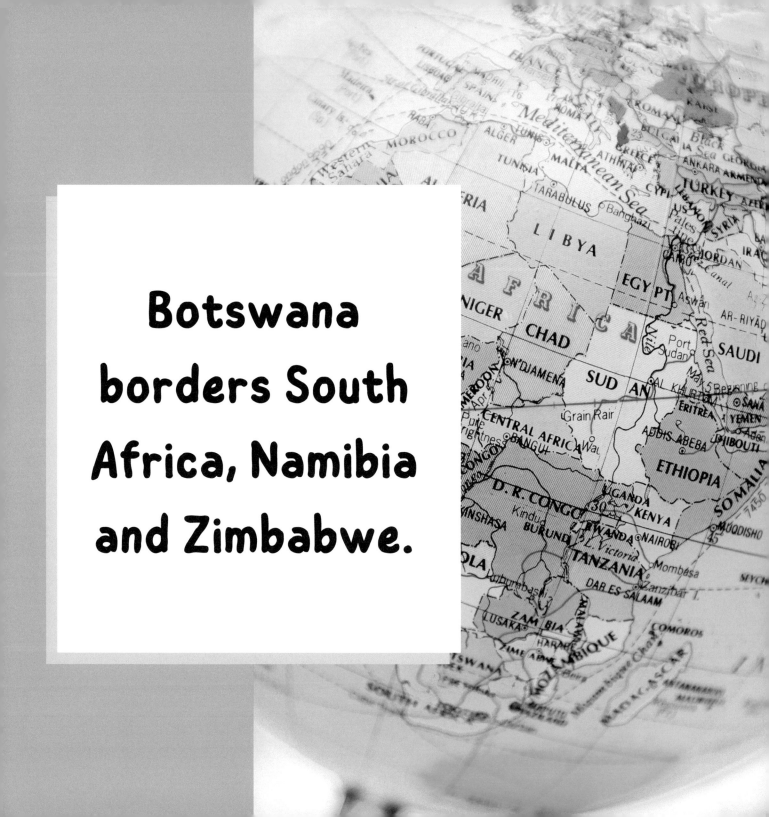

Botswana borders South Africa, Namibia and Zimbabwe.

The capital city of Botswana is Gaborone.

Gaborone, Botswana

The official languages of Botswana is Setswana and English.

Bush people of Botswana

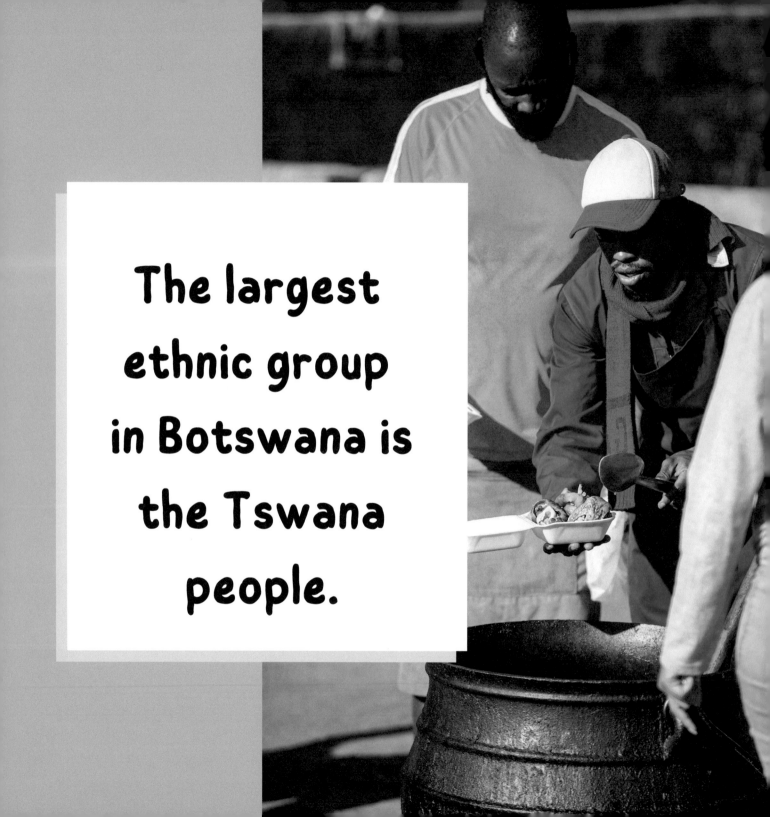

The largest ethnic group in Botswana is the Tswana people.

The Tswana people make up about 79 per cent of the population.

The motto of Botswana is 'Pula'.

Safari in Botswana

The word 'Pula' means rain.

The national anthem is 'Fatshe leno la rona'.

The country is 581,000 square kilometres.

Botswana is the world's 48th largest country.

Chobe National Park

People from Botswana are called Batswana or Motswana.

Botswana has a population of around 2 million people.

Botswana is one of the most sparsely populated countries in the world.

Botswana gained independence from the United Kingdom on 30th September 1966.

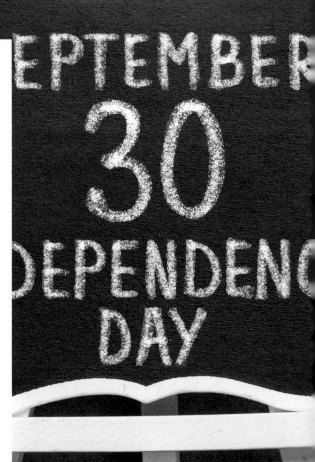

The currency of Botswana is the 'Pula'.

The largest religion in Botswana is Christianity.

Old Palapye Church, Botswana

Homo sapiens first inhibited Botswana over 200,000 years ago.

Botswana has one of the largest elephant population in Africa.

There are over 350 species of birds in Botswana.

North Botswana has one of the few remaining large populations of endangered African wild dog.

Botswana is haven for endangered species including the cheetah, brown hyena and the kori bustard.

Huge herds of zebra and wildebeest make annual migration to Botswana to find water.

Most of Botswana is flat.

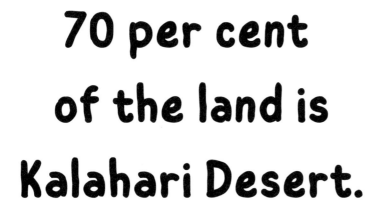

70 per cent
of the land is
Kalahari Desert.

Kalahari Desert,
Botswana

Botswana is home to the San people, who are one of the oldest tribes in the world.

The Limpopo river basin lies partly in Botswana.

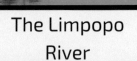

The Limpopo River

Botswana is the home of one of the world's largest salt pans, the Makgadikgadi Pan.

Makgadikgadi Pan, Botswana

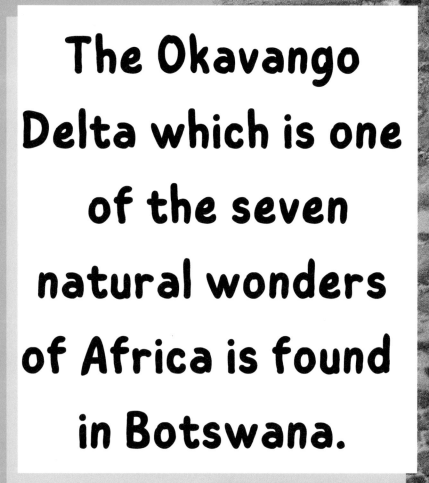

The Okavango Delta which is one of the seven natural wonders of Africa is found in Botswana.

The Okavango Delta

Botswana is Africa's oldest continuous democracy.

The economy is based largely on mining.

Botswana has rich deposits of diamonds, soda ash, copper and coal.

Botswana's climate allows for the growth of many crops such as sugarcane and cassava.

The national dish of Botswana is Seswaa.

Popular dishes in Botswana include Segwapa, Mogatla, Menoto, Braai meat and Dibete.

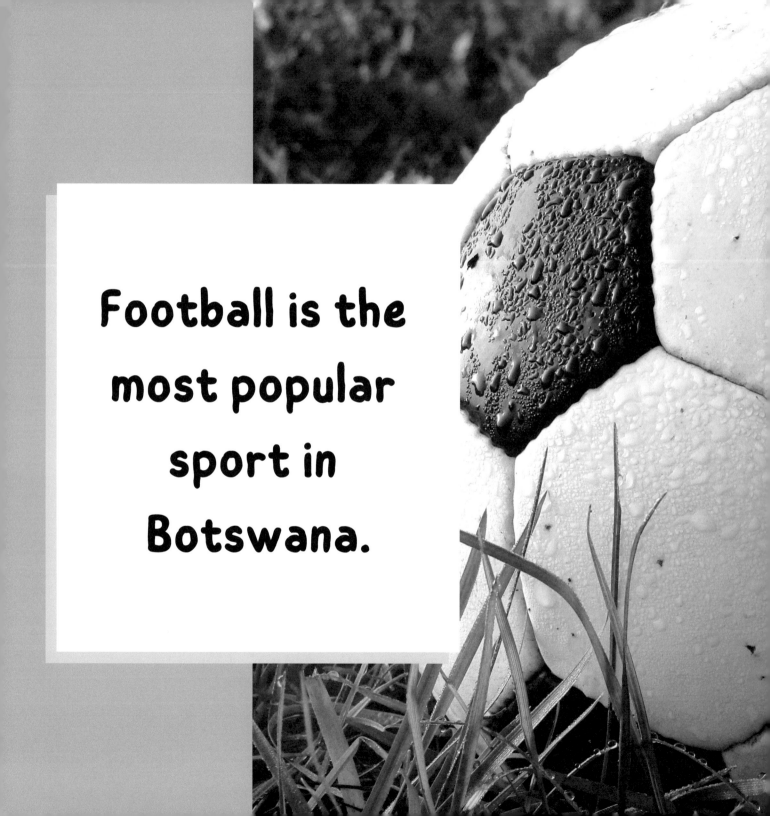

Football is the most popular sport in Botswana.

The national soccer team of Botswana is called the Zebras

WHAT WAS YOUR FAVOURITE FACT?

Made in United States
Troutdale, OR
10/01/2024

23299437R00029